Beyond Wings

Alison Lock

Indigo Dreams Publishing

First Edition: Beyond Wings
First published in Great Britain in 2015 by:
Indigo Dreams Publishing
24 Forest Houses
Halwill
Beaworthy
EX21 5UU

www.indigodreams.co.uk

ISBN 978-1-909357-83-9

British Library Cataloguing in Publication Data. A CIP record
for this book can be obtained from the British Library.

Designed and typeset in Palatino Linotype by Indigo Dreams.

Cover design by Di Carey – careydi@tiscali.co.uk
Flickr: Scareydicarey.
Author photo George Lock
Printed and bound in Great Britain by 4edge Ltd.
www.4edge.co.uk.
Papers used by Indigo Dreams are recyclable products made
from wood grown in sustainable forests following the guidance
of the Forest Stewardship Council.

above the moor
not attached to anything
a skylark singing

- Matsuo Basho

CONTENTS

Beyond Wings

On Waking

We shed our dream-skin
bottling the djinn

as fine petals reveal
the harlequin

of a Snakeshead Fritillary:
white, purple, chequered

– a new day's hue
yawning in the dew.

Oystercatchers

Our oars cut the lean
as piper pigeons coo.

On the island two trees clasp
the earth with veined roots.

Our feet dangle, drawing
heart-shapes on the tarn—

not knowing our symbols will be
read as hostile flags

until we see the semaphore of wings—
a nesting pair have taken flight,

airborne stripes of black, white,
a shock red warning

swooping in—all but striking
–scuttling—we swing a wider course.

On Black Hill

The grouse are chortling
as we three clamber and slip
and they, in that know-it-all way
at a white wedding,
chatter beneath the brims
of their whipped-up hats.
On one side of the track, on risen knolls;
the shooting boxes. No sentinels
at the butts today—their weapons arrested
hung up in the gunneries while
the beaters in their stockinged feet
dub their boots in tallow light.

We make out the rise of the hill
thickened with snow
but not that we are watched.
Silent eyes, hair ears, twitch-flighty
sizing up our dog
as he bounds the tussocks.
A buck hare, fleet as speed
flicks a 'bog cotton' tip
as we hear a yap, a yelp
on the slippery bog.
Our dog is a laughing stock
—a new subject for the grouse of Black Hill.

Peace Talks

We are at the centre of a village, a temporary green, a gathering of tents and marquees, surrounded by the towers of academia– –tall glass buildings that let in the light and through arches we glimpse new paths. Beyond the campus, far from these city walls, the firing continues. We meet to talk, to exchange ideas, to hope. We even have our own language, an idiolect of peace, where every inflection is considered. We have stopped our lives, lifted all defence, assured our differences are mutual. We wait in a circle. Holding hands. Stilled energy in motion.

lily pads float on a pond
breaking the tension

Madonna of Truro

The chatter of visitors, a sense of floating
incense that drifts the day-to-day within
the great cathedral, vaulting ascendant, encrypted
valour turned cold on stone plaques.

But I am not here to launch a crusade
as I weave through rows of stacked plastic chairs,
I find her in the darkened shadows tucked
behind a pillar, the Madonna with her Child,

niche discreet, away from prying eyes.
I wonder if she is made of polished marble
or some other blackened stone, not coal
but to my touch, she's a stilled warm ember,

her texture, the flesh of ebony wood.
I catch the scent of sweet milk as her child
nuzzles her breast. She looks at me as if to say,
'so now you have found us, leave us in peace.'

After Matins

—Reflections on Hildegard of Bingen

i

After matins
in the air
a kyrie still lingers

her long gown sweeps the lemon balm
creates a morning Heaven scent.

Bent in habit she plucks from the earth
a mandrake's silent scream (to treat a barren queen)
lady's mantle, sage for the fever sick,
rosemary and rue.

On weeding convolvulus
a black cat's tail
curlicues her gathering hands.

ii

Ordo Virtutum

The music comes from dreams
visions of a human soul
a delicate song of the Virtues
too easily crushed

'Follow the devil' they whisper
as the music turns
and twists the smoking vapour
around her simple heart.

The soul contorts, shifts,
seethes in a violent foam
until the stillness comes.
Slowly, quietly,

she enters a garden of sweetness
a robe of radiance cloaks her
with celestial love, illuminating
a mystical truth.

iii

She stands on an earthly mound under a milk sky.
Men have come to hear a woman speak.

'You craftsmen, artisans,
carpenters, stonemasons
I bid you heed instruction:

the pipes will carry water from the wells
strict measurement must be taken of all cells
the courtyard will have cloistered walks
a garden with south facing walls
at the centre our celestial home
where daily prayers will echo around a dome.

Unnerving her
the jealous Abbot whispers threats of sabotage.

To the mound each time she returns

trembling, she speaks of her vision.

iv

halo enigma
　　　encircling her face
　　　　　radiating eye lights
　　　　　　　open palms reflecting
　　　　　　　　　her shared blessings
　　　　　　　　　　　from a mystic
　　　　　　　　　script of visions
　　　　　　humbly she holds
　　　　her monastery
　　close at heart
like a secret -
　　　a holy living secret
within her
　　　hortus conclusus.

Summering

Wild geraniums, buddleia, aquilegia—all the shades of purple, mauve and pink. I hardly notice the high pitched ululation of the bees. I am passive—a spectator to the blooming. But the interloping couch grass and the fine seed heads of the barley have a will-o'-the-wisp way of entering my heart.

Nothing is ugly in the garden, not even the dead. The old cherry with the loose bark is a home for tunnelling beetles, ants and wood lice; the pear tree with its curled leaves is somehow exotic despite the rot that set in during the wet spring.

Preceded
by the tainted mewl
of winter

The Eucalyptus of Canterbury

Cradled, my feet
tune in, roots vibrate
as my rocking heels

shelve the loam,
angered ants weave
beaded manacles

around my ankles.
Silver-furred trees
crest holy spires

littering the ground
with splintered
sheaths of cinnamon

castings, heavy
with the scent
of a too-long summer.

Rain arrives, I hug
the tree, hearing the drone
of a didgeridoo.

Hexagon

If you want to hear silence, be still,

but do not ask the butterfly to freeze
or the damselfly to close its netted wings

or bid the bee to stop the nectar's flow.

Instead, take a look inside the honeycomb,
hold up a single hexagon

to a clear blue sky,
see how all six sides connect.

There is no sound,
but you will want to cry.

John Cage Says

Listen   to nothing   four minutes   plus seconds.

The drone will transform a migration
the flight of a bird on the wing.

Dip your ear in the space that opens between

the here and the rhythmic world. Chance music
a rhythm that beats for the dance

infernal white noise falls like snow.

Playground

As we drive past the park, I see children on swings, their legs kicking out, sending them higher and higher, a boy turning a roundabout, whizzing, faster and faster as a girl watches. I see a single tree, leafless branches like unsheathed bones, bending towards them in a half embrace. It is as if the sap has stopped and the tree is shunned, abandoned by the fertile rush of leaf and seed and pod and bud and all the other bursting things like meadow grass and hedge. The cries and shouts and delights from the playground echo, becoming smaller and smaller, until the park, this moment in time, has gone, out of sight, beyond the quarter light.

fledglings
not knowing
the sky is endless

Fish Bone

There's a fish bone,
a Paleozoic skeleton,
a spectre, an apparition
on a sonic scan.

Twelve weeks in vitro
and there you are,
in perfect
working order.

We stare at the bird,
the fish, made
in our dreams
on a nest of pillows.

Now, here on a screen
framed by width
of numbers, figures,
percentiles, you are

here, but not here,
temporarily submerged
in a liquid world
waiting to exchange

the sonic booms
for airborne
cries of neither
fish nor bird.

The Lizard

We are on the Cornish coast, down by the Lizard. It's a hot day, really hot. We have stopped by a hotel bar for ice water and juice. We sip our drinks, hydrate, face the sea as palm trees sway and agapanthus bow their heads. I walk towards the edge of the cliff, I look down from a great height.

feathery pampas
wind rusted crocosmia
bristling at the edge

You call me back. An echo chamber is formed between the cliffs. Like tumbleweed, children float and roll in the surf. Their voices become waves, folding in, turning, as gulls glide.

a quivering sea
blue glitter
striking at granite

We walk into the village to buy an ice-cream. The steep path falls towards a petering edge. We dare each other to look over, afraid we will want to fly. We carry on along a trail of sun cream, sand prints, a broken sandal-strap, a red bucket; discards.

with the spume
of the incoming tide
flotsam jettisoned

Lark

'They been larkin' around,' he says
as we stare at the sign that is twizzled
at a place in the fork of the road:
Coverack, Ruan Minor, Lizard.

The hedgerows are studded with stitchwort,
the blackberries green, sour to eat,
the scent of meadowsweet clears the air,
stubbled fields wane in the heat.

There is no deciphering the road sign,
the lanes look alike at the junction's T,
our brows are furrowed with questions,
our journey delayed, then we see

—that a bird in the field is rising,
it plummets, then hovers at height,
a nip in the sky with a ceaseless song
—a Cornish summer in flight.

Lifelines

We are standing on a bridge, stones glued with aged lichen—
but there are gaps, cracks, openings. Momentarily they are
filled; memories, past walks, listening, naming the times,
heaving our packs, unburdening, speaking our lives. Now we
watch the water, hear the clatter of river over rocks and on the
edge—the plosives.

trees
drop their cones
snowmelt

The Sundial

It was last October, your eightieth birthday
when the garden was turning its back to the Sun
– so you waited 'til Spring when
the rays would be strong enough for the task of counting time.

An old bird bath made an ideal plinth,
the lichen scrubbed clean from the stone pedestal
revealed a cherub:
naked, soft kneed, peep toed, unfolded wings.

You filled the bowl with cement and set the dial in line,
then you tied up the last of the daffodils,
trained the roses how to climb,
made a bed of fine tilth for the onion sets.

It must have been two o'clock when you noticed
the narrow beam of the shadow hand.
Removing your gardener's hat you went indoors
to check the time on the grandfather clock.

Migrant

Rubbed feathers stretch the wind
for those who do not make it over the sea
where tears fall from a sky
of broken wings
made brilliant by their weepings
where each journey is both old and new
along a pencilled road
leaving a sketch of half-remembered,
half-read poems.

Delayed Murmuration: No Mexican Wave

Last year, before Autumn curled the leaves
or formed a lingering blanket of neutral greys
there came a reminder of days gone by
like a swatch of holiday snaps, impossibly blue.
Already the birds were poised in migratory black, three deep
on the telegraph wires, pole to pole, waiting
for the messenger of mercury, and just
when it was time for the turn of the current on the equinox tide
something happened to change their minds.
Whether it was the unseasonal heat, the unfiltered
dusk or the abundance of sodium streetlight
at a time when we expect undulations of Mexican waves

—we don't know—

they simply stopped dusting-off their long haul wings.
Perhaps it was the way the sun spilled chilli red, tie-dying
the sky with African marigolds on a hue of Hibiscus.
Whatever: it stopped the starlings from daubing their arrow
heads
or splashing their petrol hides across our Northern sky.
Maybe those wires transmitted a secret code, broadcasting
from the churches that carved lyrebirds had escaped
from the misericords. Even the robins ceased their posturing
as they passed olive branches from one beak to another,
while timid sparrows plumped their breasts, the air cooing
with Taj Mahal dove lovers playing peek-a-boo
around the pillars of the town hall, flirting
in the lime scented air as simple songbirds harmonised.

There were no swan songs.

Shrovetide

The day is a cowl, all colours muted—mud, stone, water, even the grass is grey. We cannot speak, our breath barely flickers, our words extinguished in the damp air—just small exchanges over stiles, murmurings through brambles.

Walking side on side to the mud, inch by inch, we make our way home.

> Luminous moss
> intensifies

In the light

With every coming and going of breath
the sepia ghosts steal through the eyelets of beech
and I am Gulliver, lost
in the places where others pray.

I find no comfort in silver wares, arbours
of chaliced altars, steeples, domes, stone circles.
My sanctuary is in the soles of my feet
where earth is the spongy fodder and life exists.

My tread is the trespasser's, reined in
by old thorns, dread leaves, dead hands.
But I see brilliance through the leaves, framed
by the overhung trees, a child in the light.

Woodburner

the fish lie low
under discs
of ice slit whips
echoing through woods
rumbled hooves
halos of frost
dragged moss
logs embossed
flame for the hearth
flame for the hearth
logs embossed
dragged moss
halos of frost
rumbled hooves
echoing through woods
of ice slit whips
under discs
the fish lie low

Eye of the Heron – Summer 2012, Holmfirth (excerpt)

Gone
with the storm valley
trade wind

fair to white
as spring
heather

a summer
of wet bunting
for all

but the heron
of the vales
the Ribble and the Holme

stilled
stock solid
as rock

a hieroglyph
an ibis
poised

grey white
porcelain
plumage

stork
bittern
spoonbill, crane

in flight
a trinity, a confluence
of wing

a ministry
of airborne angel
over spire

where a brass band
plays
valley deep

refractions
of glass stained
with light

as chins tilt
eyes orbit
bright

the chime
of time
slips

into ripples
of the rivers'
sibilance.

Designs
of the intricate
twisting

leaves
falling
appliqued

a quilt
thrown
from the earth

gold
ochre, vermillion
rouge

flung
into a vast pool
of mille fleur

where
the bilberry hills
spilled

at peak
of current
bedrock, sweep

where
an S-bend neck
retracts

a gliding carnivore
harpoon bill
primed

no splash
just spit, split
sputter

a fish
a vole, rodent
swallow

– gone
with the storm valley
trade wind.

fugue

humming
on harp wires
rows of late leavers
starlings on a stave
awaiting the fulcrum
of a fickle tide
tip-to-tipping
for the fugue

Pegasus

The day is made of white and grey
a monochrome without the black
the only colour a catch of hay

hooked on a wall in a string sack
by the field gate, I lift the latch.
Quick! I step away, stand well back

miss the swinging of the swatch as
on my lips three syllables form
—in olden days I'd be a witch

for naming that of legend born
a beast of myth—there's none will say
they've seen a horse with wing and horn.

Now, when I walk the fields by day
or night, I look for unicorn
—but all I find is horse, and hay.

Her Watch

Old-fashioned, delicate,
still ticking after 80 years

a gift from her husband
for some occasion, I do not know.

Perhaps to celebrate
the birth of their first born,

or when he arrived home
after the war – a different man.

Now they are gone
his gift to her is left to me

—too precious

loaded on my wrist.
I can hardly bear the weight.

Joining up the dots

I juggle half shell to half shell.
A string of mucus
loosens, a swinging thread
drifts like a memory.

I see the tension in her arm,
folding in flour, milk, tears,
while my cutter is making
the shape of a star.

At night we look up to the loved ones,
as they join up the dots,
sketching their ploughs
and bears and dragons until —

Up there!
she points to the new arrival,
the one that pulls on the thread — still attached to our hearts.

Poppy Day

crows salute
      from boughs as
ploughs break
      the silent truce
turning earth
      raising seed
black eye
      blood red

Thirst

The weather is hotter than usual even for July—the height of our northern summer. As we walk over the hills we see a reservoir in the far distance and our conversation stops. We lick our dry lips and look around for a place to stop; to make a den in the heather, to lay down to absorb the cool earth, to eat the apples that have been bobbing in our rucksacks for miles, or just to stare up at the cool blue.

We continue over another hillock and the path widens and the ground is patched where white rags have been tucked between the ridges stretching along both sides of the valley.

flecked moors
bog cotton-grass
the snow of summer

Purple

I see a strong but indefinable shade today
like a purple filter over the whole of my life
tinted with rose-pinks from happy days, hues
of folding blues from the darker days.
Here I am on a fragile cusp, I do not know
which way I'll go but my eyes are drawn
to the indigo skies with the lapis lazuli clouds.

Kingfisher—upriver from Pulteney Bridge

Elliptical waves form our wake as we
pare the river, sprinkling the green water
with jewels of many other summers
as the reeds on both sides quiver, the trees
lean in, parched-leaves shiver, even branches
flinch at our boat's approach. Now we're almost
there—our destination—Bathhampton weir
with a toll-bridge at the turnpike Grade II
listed, the tour guide says, regaling us
with tales, but my attention is drawn to
the tip of a peacock's feather that now
adorns a tiny bird in a dull tree.

Guiding Lights

In this dream I follow
the marks made by the sea-stars.

I watch their
flaccid tendrils crossing
the tide-line where the curling
waves shoal.

I sail on a boat of glass.
Below, I see
the clutter of
a city on the ocean floor.

Aerials are breaking
the surface
beacons of light are blinking
from the skylights

their bright orbits
guiding me over the sea.

Isle of Iona

The ferry from Mull is to-ing and fro-ing all day long, bringing the visitors, who, like the over-summering birds, have come for a temporary roost. These seekers of tranquility, pilgrims who yearn for the cloistered incense of the Abbey, follow a trail of holy souvenirs. A sign in Gaelic says all who visit will return three times.

> at the nunnery
> bone-stones crumble
> Reformation continues

Later, we look back at Iona from Mull. Fast clouds are skittering across the sky and the sidewinding-rain flecks the window pane. The placid sheep are chewing the grass, heaving under thick lanolin coats. They seem unaware of the oncoming storm as the far mountains retreat under a pall of cloud, a shroud. Out on the darkening blue is the jewel, Iona, awaiting a Viking slaughter. A slash of rain and we are left with the dripping grey of sand, rock, sea, sky, and grass, where even harebells are mute amongst the stony outcrops.

The skerries are indistinguishable—somewhere between water and air.

> the artist
> outlines the sea, sky, and earth
> – no-man's land

Affirmation

A summer's night, one of those before-a-breaking-storm nights, when the dark is stifling as it falls and slips through the open skylight. Above me, a sheer formation of stars trail the sky; a white linen nightshift flung from east to west on a northern hemisphere. I try to count them but in my sleep-unslaked state I don't know which ones I have already counted. So, I start again from the beginning until I am confused and all they do is sparkle and tease. What I would do for forty of their winks.

on the branches
pigeons slumber
in silhouette

The Traveller

I am

a traveller.

I make my home

in rented rooms, in tents

or caravans. I carry this heart

and mind wherever I go. I surround

myself with reminders of my life, treasures

like the one given me by a child; a piece of red

glass found on a roadside and when I look through it

I see a world made rosy with tinted triangles. A small white

cube fits in the corner of my case; my wind-up radio that tells me

about a world outside of my own. I have a scarf of velvet fabric that is

like the touch of the lover I miss. I have my pens and my paper for catching the

words, to describe every footprint I see in the sand. I am a traveller and this is my room.

The Crossing

In the shaded area
of a venn diagram
that intersects
if only tangentially
we skip a dance,
apologise
to each other,
when all that matters
is
that when we pass
—we smile

Vienna

I almost missed the shop with its narrow window, a mere yard of glass, cafes on either side. Shoes. Perched, pitched, not paired, nor practical. Seamless, fine leather, displayed singly, as if they are jewels. Brogues for the perfect bound.

window reflections
my hand on the
schumacher's door

I walk along a narrow path where the air is filled with the acidic scent of fresh spray-paint. On one side is a high wall that runs along the edge of a rail track. Graffiti fills the old stonework with the snakes and dots of a cryptic language. His work done, the artist clips the tops onto the cans and stands back to admire each swirl, every sweep, bordered in black; feathered, exact.

through caged arches
a train growls

fibonacci mist

I

write

your name

in the mist

reveal the garden

where forsythia flowers in

a fountainous spray and the once pruned arch of privet

sprigs and curlicues like the cat's tail that now frames the overgrown path, and with my sleeve

I rub at my breath and see the lawn as wilderness;

plantain heads, bindweed, knotgrass, dark

shadows under our

tree where the

bluebells

still

bloom

Leichtenstein Gardens

A rose with stone petals; a garden within a city of all things monumental where a stream spouts eternally from the cherub's pail and stone pillars pocked by history make elegant statues, where even the trees are ornate, clipped to fit, boxed along an avenue. The pond reflects every colour of sky, an earring dropped by a careless god.

> into the ornamental pond
> I dip my feet
> autumn leaves on marble

I hear a gasp behind me. On the path lies a rose, a single red. A girl in a pair of broken flip flops has picked it up and she is offering it to me.

> my feet are weights
> a pavement of stone slabs

Yin/Yang

The sun is a splinter
in the grass.

A blackbird pecks at seed
luring a jay.

The moon is the blade
of a scythe

reflected on the wings
of moths.

Kiss

We are in limelight
treading a pebbled stage

our esses are stolen
by the waves

as silver tongues
lap the shore

our eyes switch
in the strip-light

our lips are
the full moon.

Early Morning, Isle of Gigha

Droplets of water on the bell tent offer themselves to the sky but the sun is slow to accept. Eventually they will evaporate, but for now, they are glowing crystal beads strewn across the tents, the cars, the field. I emerge from the flaps of the dewy canvas, blinking. Out in the bay, the sea folk are fettling their boats, putting away their balers after the storm. The placid moon of last evening gave no warning of what was to come. These old moorings will soon be replaced by a new pontoon for more yachts to gain a temporary purchase on the sea—time enough for the crews to refuel and re-replenish their stocks or amble towards the hotel bar.

blue flame
on the primus stove
a kettle whistles

Along the single road that leads to the ferry dock, a truck rumbles over a cattle grid as the first ferry of the day moves through the deep water channel from the South Pier. There are no passengers at the dock, not this early, in the holiday season. I look out over the bay from this campsite by the loch. A gull is watching from one of the moored boats, and another rises from a mast as a tanoy twitches into life—a safety announcement begins—'This is Caledonia...'

The water is felted glass, reflecting the stilled clouds of an unruffled sky. The curlews in their sand nests warble, the oystercatchers pewit across the sky. By the rocks, the seaweed prickles in the wash, bladderwrack pops, seagrass ripples like luxury velvet, seed heads bowed.

undercurrents
ripple the slip surface
a sleek guillemot dips

Under the wooden pier, roped in, hitch-knotted, in a creel: three lobsters. A few yards away from the Boathouse restaurant is a blackboard—*On the Menu Today—Fresh Lobster*. Already the 'four' has been crossed out, replaced by the faint curls of 'three'. Swaying in their tidal hammock.

gulls glide
over the rocks
my seat on the edge

Diving

As we walk towards the lighthouse at Neist Point on the Isle of Skye, the heavens change from a brooding morass to one where shards of sunlight shoot from the west, peeling each cloud. The wind is bitter, biting at my ears and nose, but even so, I can taste the air—unadulterated by the taint of city; diesel, smog, smoke. By the time we reach the headland, a rainbow is fingering a multi-coloured arc across the sky and all the clouds have fled. The white thumb of the lighthouse stands before us at the edge of the world. On the opposite headland there are streamers hanging over the cliffs; ribboned slivers of crystal water that rush and plunge down and down the steep sides of sheer rock as if they cannot wait to join the ocean a hundred feet below. I am used to the inland rivers, the mountain pools, the gentle splutter over rock, or above the weirs where the water remains so still. But here, all sources have rebelled; springing and sprinting towards the westernmost tip of the island, careless, unimpeded, falling into the welcoming arms of the sea.

droplets from a spring
somersaulting
to the beckoning moon

One for sorrow

Black, white,
crossing our path
a swatch against the grey-green
of leaves, branches, sky.

I worry,

search for another,
a pairing, a joy.

But today is a sad day.

Osmosis

I am the river,
above are the swallows
that skull and arc the wind
wings reaching for my thoughts
like paper scraps that play the air
and land to float downstream.

They are your words
that fall upon my liquid skin,
droplets of ink, words that blot
frayed with feathered edges
essences absorbed.
Osmosis.

Smoke

The touch of flame on wax
pooling on the table,
spittle on finger and thumb
sizzling, leaving

a fine grey line,
a detail—rising in the dark.

Acknowledgements

With thanks to the editors of the following publications where versions of these poems have appeared.

In the (Quarter) Light, John Cage Says – Southlight
Madonna of Truro – Pennine Platform
Guiding Lights, Migrant, Poppy day – The Lake
Playground, Lifelines, Vienna – Haibun Today
Hexagon – Reach
Delayed Murmuration: no Mexican Wave – Off the Coast Literary Journal
Her Watch (The Weight) – Westward Quarterly
The Traveller, Purple – Sarasvati
Shrovetide, One for Sorrow – Lyrical Passion Poetry e-zine

After Matins – Hildegard visions & inspiration – ed Gabriel Griffin 2014
Joining up the dots – Heart Shoots – ed Ronnie Goodyer 2013
The Sundial – Rhyme and Reason, Rennie Grove Hospice Care Calendar 2012

Eye of the Heron – with thanks to Holmfirth Arts Festival for the opportunity of 'Poet in Residence 2012'.

Indigo Dreams Publishing
24 Forest Houses
Halwill
Beaworthy
EX21 5UU